MW01289923

Fresh Start
For Dads

(Second Edition)

Reconnecting After
Prison & Absenteeism

By Delonso Barnes

To all the dads that are trying to get it right this time around. I pray for you and your families.

And to my big brother, keep your head up.

Terms and Conditions
LEGAL NOTICE

Table Of Contents

Introduction 1

The Family's Burden of Incarceration 4

Assisting Your Family With Coping 6

Answering Your Child's Difficult Questions 14

Conversation Starters With Your Children .. 16

50 Ways To Improve Your Relationships 20

Q & A with Yourself 31

Personal Development 36

100+ Daily Activities And Mindsets
Challenges 73

Things To Keep In Mind 84

Getting Work 91

What Is Financial Empowerment? 106

Starting Over Quotes 136

Positive Affirmations 138

Post Release Checklist 141

10 Helpful Resource Links 142

The Seven Essential Steps To A Successful
Life 143

The First 45 Days Journal...............................146

The Author...192

Introduction

Dads, just because you are incarcerated and haven't seen your children in a while, doesn't not mean you are not still responsible for the safety, health, education and financial-being of your child and family as a whole. Being away from your family is difficult and makes it seem impossible to do one of the most important duties as a father. Be present. Be being present isn't just about being there in the physical form. I hope and pray this book will enable you to connect with your family while still in prison and find balance in life on the outside.

I am Delonso Barnes, Director of Daddy Everyday Inc. and Author of *Daddy Everyday, Rewriting The Black American Dad Story*. This isn't a book based on my experience in prison. Through the research and writing process of *Daddy Everyday* and working with fathers at schools and churches, I learn some things about the difficulty of fathering from prison and life after prison. My goal with this handbook is to empower you not as ex-con, but as a man and a father. This book will educate you on connecting and bonding with your family while on the inside. This book will as well assist you on getting your life on track on the outside.

If you are determined to get yourself together and willing to go through the struggles that will inevitably come, then this book will serve you well. This book is designed to be a quick read. It's the actions required of you that will be the time consuming and beneficial to you.

Please understand that the struggle you will experience will at times seem unfair and too difficult overcome. But you can and you must. Others were affected by the decisions you made that lead you to now to need this book. Understand and accept their frustration and maybe anger towards you. People are going to judge you on your past; your goal should be to create a promising present and better tomorrow. This way your today will one day be your new past.

The fact that you are reading this book is a step in the right direction and shows that you are making the positive effect to be a better man...father.

Also, please don't let this be the last book, handbook or brochure you read on getting yourself together before and after release. Make it your mission to get a Fresh Start.

As you can tell this book will be based on incarcerated fathers, then absentee fathers. However, the principals and tools are still the same.

The Family's Burden of Incarceration

Before we can venture into the things you can do to be a connected father and spouse/partner, we must discuss the negative impact your incarceration has on you children and family.

Research shows that children are the ones severely impacted by their father's incarceration. Children with incarcerated fathers are more likely to show poor conduct or grading in school, develop substance abuse, perform serious delinquent acts and worse, become incarcerated themselves. Spouses/Partners feel abandoned, frustrated with the sole responsibility of parenthood and overwhelmed by the financial obligations.

The longer you are in, the greater the distance that will form between you and your family. As well as the deeper the wounds will become, which will make it that much more difficult to repair them. That's why it's important to act now and be consistent with your actions.

Incarcerated dads who have positive family support and relationships do not return to prison as much as those who lack this support. Studies have shown that children of inmates with negative family relationships are seven times more likely to end up incarcerated. That's why it's important to keep this incarceration period in mind when creating and maintaining the family bond.

Assisting Your Family With Coping

In some cases, the parental guardians to the children while you are away maybe your spouse, partner, parent or a family member. So for clarity and consistency, we will refer to the one taking care of your children as parental guardian. One of the most important relationships during this incarceration period will be between you and the parental guardian. It is vital that you have a healthy relationship and communication with the parental guardian.

Prison will have its own unique issues that your family members and mainly the parental guardian will not understand. To be honest it's not their responsibility to understand, they have their own issues to deal with on the outside. Don't throw your frustration about your situation and take out your anger on them. Remember you are the one that put yourself in this situation. Believe it or not, you are more responsible for helping your family to adjust than they are for helping you adjust.

Over the next couple of pages, let's breakdown how you can assist your parents, spouse/partner and children cope with your incarceration.

Parents

Being the parent of a child who is incarcerated can bring many different emotions and struggles to the parent's life. Guilt and the feeling that they should have done more for their child is just a couple of the struggles. Sadness and fear for the well being of their child. Embarrassment and shame of having a child that went down the wrong path. And to be honest, they have the right to feel however they want to feel. You need to instill confidence in them that this is the end of your downward spiral and not the beginning. Take full responsibility of your actions that lead you into this situation. Talking about the positive that will come out of this situation will ease your parents stress and begin the building of confidence and support for you.

Please be aware, that you parents may feel angry with you and your actions. This will be a confusing time for them, emotionally. Your positive actions and simple time will be needed for them to move from the anger stage. Don't' be surprised if this stage doesn't seem like it's going to end. Accept it if they show these feelings because they are normal. Allow them to talk straight with you about their feelings.

A common theme you will see in this book is that you will be the one comforting, reassuring and supporting your family members.

Spouse/Partner (Parental Guardian)

Dealing with having a spouse/partner incarcerated, is a lot to handle. Physical and emotional separation is just part of what she has the burden to deal with. Whatever you were with her in terms of a healthy relationship, you will have to go all out to maintain that relationship, partnership and bond. Below are a couple of things you can do to maintain and build on your bond with her. Keep in mind you know what she likes and what she doesn't like, so tailor these ideas to the liking of her. Not your preference or convenience.

Staying Connected Suggestions:
- Write letters daily or weekly at the least.
- Encourage her to visit, don't demand.
- Make talking on the phone special, not a financial burden.

- If she has friends or family that visits the prison, encourage her to visit when they visit their loved ones. This way she doesn't have to come to such an intimidating place alone.
- Read the books she is reading. You can talk about it with her and share your thoughts.
- Inquire and brainstorm about her financial well-being. Don't wait till it frustrates her.

Remember that despite the fact that you are locked away, it is still your relationship and you have a role to play. You need to control any anger you feel when she is not around when you phone her, or when she misses a visit. You may also get upset if she has to make an emergency decision about an important matter without your input. Keep your feelings in check when it comes to the decisions that are made in your physical appearances. You are entitled to express your feelings about how she is handling family matters, how often she visits or the communication (or lack thereof) but you should not let the anger get the best of you. Your decisions put the both of you in this situation.

Children

A child will feel many different emotions when their dad is in prison. Confused, fearful, abandon and sad are just a couple of the emotions they will feel. They may even feel a sense of loss like a loved one passing. The parental guardian will be busy holding everything down and may not have the time to correctly deal with the emotional rollercoaster the child may be experiencing. That's why it's very important that you and the parental guardian must be on the same page and work together to assist the child get through this situation.

Be aware that one emotion that may occur is anger. The child may feel anger towards you, and may not want anything to do with you. The child will associate the pain they are feeling with you causing it. The matter in which you were imprisoned will play a part in how the child will react to your incarceration.

Shame and embarrassment may be experienced, depending on the age of the child. They may be teased or even bullied if the other children are aware of it. This combined with all the different emotions they are experiencing can be a lot for a child to handle, at any age. You and the parental guardian have to keep this in mind and strategize for it.

Performing poorly in school, acting differently, fighting, bad dreams and committing crimes or clear signs that your child is negatively affected by the incarceration. You won't be able to see the daily signs and that is why it's imperative that the parental guardian is aware of daily condition of the child.

Bullet Points On Helping Children Cope

- Don't sugarcoat the fact that you are in prison. Help them understand you were wrong and prison is how you will make it right.
- Make sure your child knows he or she is loved.
- Encourage your child to communicate their emotions.
- Make visitation an option if it is indeed an option.
- Do right by the parental guardian as best as you can. You don't want the parental guardian bad mouthing you in front of your child.

- Always have a cheerful goodbye. Visits, calls and in letters be cheerful and optimistic.
- Ask open-ended questions to assist children with expressing themselves.

Notes

_____

_____

_____

_____

_____

_____

_____

_____

_____

_____

_____

_____

_____

_____

_____

_____

_____

_____

_____

_____

Answering Your Child's Difficult Questions

Your child will need understanding to why you're gone. Answer their questions truthfully, and here are ways you can do so and in ways that they will understand.

Where are you? "I'm in prison (jail if applicable). When adults break the law, they are sent to prison. This is not your fault, it is a result of the bad choices I made and this is my punishment for it."

Will I get to see you? "You can visit me in prison once in a while. Your parental guardian will let you know when. We will write each other often and talk on the phone to keep in touch."

Or

"We may not be able to see each other; however, we can write each other often and talk on the phone to keep in touch."

When will you be home? "I won't be home for a while, this is a part of my punishment for breaking the law. However, I'm waiting for more information and I will let you know when I find out. I'm thinking about you every day and can't wait to come home to see you."

Conversation Starters With Your Children

If you are finding it hard to have a conversation with your children, then use these 30 conversation starters to get you going.

1. What did you do this week?
2. What was something fun you did this week?
3. Did you see anyone this week that you haven't seen for a while?
4. Do you have any exciting stories to tell from the past week?
5. What is your favorite time of the year?
6. If you could receive one thing in the whole world as a present right now, what would it be?
7. What do you want to be when you get older? Why?
8. What do you like to spend your allowance on?
9. What are you studying in school right now in Math? Social Studies? Science?
10. What is your least favorite thing to study?

11. Do you have lots of homework to do each night?

12. Who is your best friend?

13. What do you like to do for fun?

14. Do you play sports? Which ones?

15. What is your favorite thing to do on the weekend?

16. Do you prefer to spend your time inside or outside?

17. What do you do when you get home from school?

18. What is your favorite TV show?

19. What is your favorite movie ever?

20. What is your favorite book?

21. What is your favorite place to eat?

22. What kind of music do you like?

23. What is your favorite song right now?

24. What types of things do you pray for?

25. Do you like going to church?

26. When you think of God, how do you picture him?

27. Do you tell other people about Jesus?

28. Are you doing the right things so you don't end up incarceration??

29. How are you feeling about my incarceration?

Jot Down More Questions

_____

_____

_____

_____

_____

_____

_____

_____

_____

_____

50 Ways To Improve Your Relationships

1. Be yourself. Authenticity is the key to growing a relationship. If you cannot be yourself then you end up playing a charade the ultimately will end badly for you.

2. Be honest. No one likes being lied to and a relationship build upon lies will create an environment of distrust. It is better to be honest and upfront, and then try to weasel out of like later on.

3. Know your values. Spend time examining the type of person that you are and the type of person that you would like to be. If these ideas are not congruent with your current relationships then it is time to do some self-examination.

4. Schedule Time. Relationships take work. It is important to schedule time with those that you care about. It shows them that they are important to you. It also ensures that you both have time to stay connected throughout the business of life.

5. Touch. The power of touch is amazing. A hug, handshake, holding hands, or even a kiss when appropriate can make all the difference in the world. Reach out and touch someone.

6. Create space. Everyone needs space and space is not a bad thing. It gives a person their own area to be themselves and to be an individual.

7. Learn to listen. An active listener is focused on what the other person is saying and is not concentrating on their own snappy comeback.

8. Learn how to be heard. Good speakers are able to order their thoughts and emotions in ways that can be understood. Speak in small segments and ask for feedback to see if the listener understands you.

9. Know the differences. Men and women are different. Moms and dads are different. Find our what those differences are and celebrate them. Differences make life interesting and exciting.

10. Give space. Know when to give your loved one the space they need to cool down after an argument. Let them know that you are there for them when they are ready to talk, but do not pursue them.

11. Give time. Dedicate yourself to spending quality and quantity time with those that you care about. Money is fleeting, but time can be controlled and given.

12. Avoid debates. To most issues there are two sides and never the twain shall meet. Learn what is important and what you can agree to disagree about.

13. Remember that you're on the same team. If you approach topics and discussions with the thought in mind that you both have to win for one of you to win, it will help both of you gain insight and understanding to the other.

14. Create shared traditions. Find something that you can do together that neither one of you bring from your home. Make it just yours.

15. Use the element of surprise. A surprise kiss, card, or act of kindness can cover a multitude of sins.

16. Laugh together. Laughing not only releases various amounts of dopamine, but it also relives stress and create a shared moment.

17. Share emotions. Many arguments can be avoided if you share how something made you feel with the person you care about. Feelings drive actions.

18. Cuddle time. Spend time getting close and enjoying each other. A movie and popcorn can create great cuddle opportunities.

19. Do things just because. Do not keep score, returning good action for good action. Do something for the one you care about just because you can, without any strings attached.

20. Have a special greeting. Guys have special handshakes;
girls often kiss checks or hug. Find a special way to greet your loved ones that show that they are individually valued by you.

21. Passion. Sex is important in a relationship. Ask your partner what turns him or her on the most. Share fantasies. The best place to do this is NOT in the bedroom, but while you are out for a walk or working in the yard.

22. Learn about your partner. Interview them as if you were going to write a biography about them.

Ask about their childhood, favorite teachers and the like.

23. Write them a letter. And mail it. Everyone loves to get mail, and everyone loves it even more to get mail from someone they care about. Just let them know you are thinking about them. It need not be fancy.

24. Show affection. First, ask your partner what affection is to them. There is no right or wrong answer here. Then, try to fill that need for affection for them.

25. Tell others what you like about them. We often only share what we like about people at their funeral after they are dead. Spend time each day sharing with people you care about what exactly you like about them. Be specific.

26. Compliment the other person. Compliments do not build a strong relationship, but they sure can keep it from squeaking. Be honest and be nice.

27. Find their special need and fill it. Everyone has one or two special needs that they value more than any other need. Find out that need in your partner then seek to be the one they can

come to get it filled.

28. Be kind. Sounds simple, and obvious, but we are often kinder to strangers than we are to those we care about because we do not want to seem rude. Be kind to those you care about
first, the others in your life can wait.

29. Find a hobby to share. Having an activity that you can share will create shared memories and moments that can carry you through tough times.
30. Find out their love language. People try to express their love in different ways, some by service, some by touch, and others by their words.

31. Read a book together. It can even be the same book. One highlights in blue the other in pink. Things shared that are important to both are in purple, now discuss!

32. Share childhood moments. Most people have moments in their childhood that were significant to them. Take turns sharing such moments and enjoy the closeness that it brings.

33. Share responsibilities. Help each other out and lend a hand. There is no competition or score keeping in a relationship. It is a team effort!

34. Buck tradition, find a good fit. If one likes to do the dishes or one likes to stay home and the other likes to work, so be it. Do not worry about what society says one person should or
should not do. Find out what works best for you, then do it.

35. Say you're sorry. The infamous words we long to hear and are afraid to utter. These three words can quickly deflate any argument, especially if said in sincerity and love.

36. Take care of yourself physically. Know when you need to take a break, get some rest or get a bit to eat. Relationships work 100% better when both partners are well rested and well fed.

37. Take care of yourself mentally. Everyone has a mental breaking point. Know yours and share that point with your partner. Let them know when you need some space and what
they may need to do or not do to help you out.

38. Take care of yourself emotionally. When emotions run wild, all logic is out the window. It is healthy to cry, to be angry, disappointed, and frustrated. Just do not hold it all in and let it all out at the same time.

39. Face spirituality together. Often this is the one thing couples discuss last. Whether you share beliefs with your partner or not, this is a discussion that is a must.

40. Leave baggage behind. It is okay to share things from the past, but drudging up old skeletons is no way to build a relationship. Leave your past behind you.

41. Create realistic expectations. Share with the one you care about your expectations for the relationship. Then as them to do the same. Then discuss which ones might be far fetched and which ones might be closer to reality.

42. Create a warm fuzzies box or folder. Keep cards, letters and mementoes from your relationship in a box or folder that is easily accessible. This will help you through those rough times.

43. Control anger. Do not let anger control you. When you feel yourself getting anger, let your partner know what is going on for you and call a time out. Then return to the conversation when you have had a chance to cool off.

44. Control finances. Children, sex, and finances are the top three reasons couples get divorced. Budget together as a team. Share the burden and responsibility.

45. Forgiveness. Forgive and be forgiven. No one can forget the past, but you can stop holding it against them. Learn from the past and move on.

46. Learn to fight a good fight. Fights are not always bad things. Refrain from name calling, putting down, and needling sensitive areas of the other person. It ups the ante so to speak.

47. Find mentors. Look for people who exemplify the type of relationship that you want. Ask them how they do it and see if
they will help you do the same.

48. Family history. Overview each other's family history. Understanding leads to empathy.

49. Keep in touch. By email or phone or through notes, let each know that you are thinking about the other throughout the day. Just a quick I'm thinking of you will suffice.

50. No jealousy allowed. Jealousy will rip a relationship apart quicker than a starving man on

a Christmas ham. Talk about your feelings, rather then let them brew until they turn into jealousy.

What three tips are you are already really effective in?

_____

_____

_____

_____

_____

_____

What three tips do you need to improve in?

_____

_____

_____

_____

_____

_____

_____

Q & A with Yourself

Who will be picking me up from the gate and where will you go?

_____

_____

_____

When will I check in with parole or probations?

_____

_____

_____

Where will I be staying? How do I feel about living there?

_____

_____

_____

How will I support myself?

_____

_____

_____

What steps do I need to get a job? Or get
financial assistance?

_____

_____

_____

Where will my emotional support come from?

_____

_____

_____

_____

What are my drug and alcohol prevention plans? (If applicable)

_____

_____

_____

What type of social life will I have?

_____

_____

_____

How am I going to make it on my own and stay free?

_____

_____

_____

_____

_____

Do I have the right mindset to make it on the outside? Why do I think so?

_____

_____

_____

What will I do for transportation?

_____

_____

_____

What elements on the outside should I avoid?

_____

_____

_____

_____

Who am I going to contact for legal, mental and housing assistance?

_____

_____

_____

_____

_____

_____

_____

_____

Personal Development

Methods of Managing Your Anger

Whenever we lose our temper, we are in real danger of damaging relationships and close ties with the people that we love. Words shouted or things thrown in anger can often be extremely hurtful to our loved ones, and it can be difficult for them to understand exactly what went wrong to trigger the reaction. Eventually, they will just stop trying and it will get more and more difficult to forgive and forget. Managing anger is extremely important, not just for you, but for everyone around you. The first important step towards managing anger is to
actually realize that you have a problem. If you look back over situations, which have made you angry in the past, it is very likely that you will realize that your loss of control actually made the situation much worse, and not better. This is an important realization for you to make when you acknowledge that you have a problem
and need to do something about it. If you feel yourself getting angry just take time out to stop, think about the situation and try to figure out just why you are getting angry. Very often the real cause of the anger is nothing to do with the

present situation, and pent up frustrations from work can overspill into your home life causing misery and upset for your loved ones which they have no control over.

Once you realize what is truly causing the anger, the next important step in managing anger is to try and fix it. This is where you may really need to bite the bullet and communicate with the source of your anger. It may be that someone at work does something which really winds you up, but by talking about it the situation can be changed successfully, they probably won't even know that they are doing it. Sometimes just be communicating problems you can actually remove the source of your anger and live a much more peaceful life.

A Good Communication Technique

Human beings are social beings and we are interacting with people every day of our life. Often, our happiness depends a great deal on how the interactions with each person turn out.

This is especially true of those whom we care about e.g. in close friendships as well as in marriage. However, because each personality we deal with is unique and presents its own challenges, managing the myriad of relationships requires us to consciously observe the process and impact of our interactions so that we continue to gain knowledge, understanding and experience in developing relationships in a positive way.

I have realized that to have good management of relationships, we need to be assertive and honest in sharing our thoughts, feelings and concerns. However, this needs to be done in a way that does not provoke the other party, but is instead respectful and encourages both parties to listen to each other. A good way to do this is through the communication technique of "I" Messages. In "I" messages, statements are made about ourselves, how we feel and our concerns, and what actions of the other party has led to the concerns. "You" messages focus on the other person and would usually lead the other party to become defensive unless the "You" message is a positive statement of the other person. For example, a husband or wife is waiting for the return of the spouse and when the spouse returns, this might greet him or her: "You are always coming home late!"

"Why can't you come back earlier?" This "You" message leads to the spouse feeling blamed and attacked and the ensuing communication would likely not be an amiable one. In a conflicting situation, "You" message focuses on attacking the other person. As a result, the primary issues are pushed aside. In contrast, in this same scenario, an "I" message would look like this: "I feel rather lonely while waiting for you to come home. I'm concerned that you are often home late and I get rather frustrated wondering when you're going to be home." In this statement therefore, the speaker shares his or her feelings and concerns. The clear communication of the concern is a good starting point for both parties to work out what can be done about it. "I" messages are effective because the focus is on the issue or concern and not on the other person. The sharing of the speaker's feelings can also lead to more trust in the relationship as it shows the speaker is willing to look within himself or herself and take responsibility for his or her feelings. In fact, generally in most interactions, my opinion is that the use of "I" messages is always superior to "You" messages and is a more respectful way of communicating. So, even when expressing positive feelings, a "You" message: "You look good in this dress", could be enhanced by "I" messages: "I'm so happy to see you. I remember all the fun we used to have.

Generally, there are three parts to an "I" message:
I feel _____ (express your feeling)
when you _____ (describe the action that
affects you or relates to the feeling) because
_____ (explain how the action affects
you or relates to the feeling)

The order in which the 3 parts are expressed is
usually not important. Sometimes a fourth part
might be added. This states our preference for
what we would like to take place instead.

Examples of more "I" messages: "I get very
anxious when you raise your voice at me because
it makes me feel like I've done something very
wrong. Could you please not raise your voice
when we talk?" "I'm so happy you're learning to
cook because then I'll know you can prepare your
own meal when I'm unable to be home in time to
cook."

"When you take so long talking to your friend on
the phone, I'm concerned that there might be
urgent calls that cannot come through. Also, I feel
frustrated, as I would like to spend more time
with you. How about asking your friend to call at
another time, when I am not around."

Use of "I" messages might not come naturally to
most people initially. However, with practice, you
will be surprised at how you will begin to like

this communication approach, especially when you begin to experience the good result of better quality interactions and more harmonious relationships.

How To Have Those Difficult Conversations

Is there a conversation you've been putting off? Is there a coworker or family member with whom you need to talk to– but don't? Maybe you've tried and it didn't turn out as you had hoped. Or maybe you fear that talking will only make things worse. Whatever the reason, you feel stuck and you'd like to free up that energy for more useful purposes. One of the most common reasons I hear in my workshops for not holding difficult conversations is that people don't know how to begin. Here are a few conversation openers I've picked up over the years and used many times. I'd like to discuss something with you that I think will help us work together better.

I think we may have different ideas about _____. When you have some time, I'd like to talk about it.

I'd like to hear your thoughts on _____. Do you have a minute?

I need your help with what just happened (or - I need your help with _____). Can we talk?

I'd like to see if we might reach a better understanding about _____. I really want to hear your thoughts on this.

All of these openers help to create an environment of respect and mutual purpose. You can say almost anything as long as you maintain these two critical conditions.

Practice, Practice, Practice

The art of conversation is like any art - with continued practice you acquire skill and ease. You, too, can create better working and family relationships, ease communication problems, and improve the quality of your environment. Yes, I know all of this sounds cheesy, but can probably ease tension in difficult times.

Here are 3 tips to get you started.
1) A successful outcome will depend on two things: how you are and what you say. How you are (centered, supportive, curious, problem-solving) will greatly influence what you say.

2) Know and return to your purpose at difficult moments.

3) Practice the conversation before holding the real one, either mentally or with a friend. Try out different scenarios and visualize yourself handling each with ease. Envision the outcome you're hoping for.

Remember that if you can find a mutual purpose for holding the conversation, and if you extend and maintain respect, you should be fine.

Time Management

1. Realize time management is a myth. Many want to squeeze too much into one day. Coming to the realization that there are only 24 hours in a day and that one can only fit so much into those hours releases one from the worries and anxieties of things that are yet to be done.

2. Find out where you're wasting time. Conduct a complete time examination. Walk through your day in 15 minutes intervals, writing down what you are doing and for how long.

3. Create time management goals. Having clear goals will guide you through the process of

getting control of your time. The best way to start is with pen and paper in hand and write out what you want more time to do.

4. Implement a time management plan. Just like a budget guides money spending, a time management plan will guide how you can use your time.

5. Use time management tools. There are thousands of time management tools available today. The best is daily or weekly planners. Other options are online calendars such as Google Calendar or Outlook.

6. Prioritize ruthlessly. Learn to cut out what is not important to you. Make a list of all the things that you need to get done, then think through each one and decide if it is worth your time or not. If not, cut it from the list.

7. Learn to delegate. Look at your to do list and see what can be handed off to other people, a spouse a coworker or a friend.

8. Establish routines and stick to them. Find your rhythm in life. Learn what time you need to go to bed, what time is best to wake up and find

specific times to do daily tasks, such as checking email and filing.

9. Set time limits for tasks. Time can get away from you really quickly if you do not have a set amount of time for a task.

10. Organize your systems. Do you use several email addresses? Several online programs? Bookmark often visited websites or put them on your explorer tool bar.

11. Don't waste time waiting. If you find yourself waiting for things to get done, bring work along with you, or even a good book that you have wanted to read. Getting an oil change? Bring something to work on.

12. Get a planner. There are many types of planners out there today, some of the better ones out line each day of the week in 15-minute intervals, as well as included a full page monthly calendar. Once you find one you like, use it.

13. Differentiate between urgent and vital. Urgent are things that are due soon, but may not be life or death. Vital are things that may or may not be urgent, but that you absolutely must do.

14. Schedule your priorities do not prioritize your schedule. Take charge of what you have before you. You have the power to decided what you do and when.

15. Time journal for two weeks, giving account for every 15 or 30 minutes of time. This will help you see where your time is going and what takes up most of your time.

16. Learn to say no. This is your greatest ally. Practice saying no in polite but firm ways. You are no one's doormat. Decide what you are going to do, then do not get distracted by other tasks that people may want you to do for them.

17. Learn what drives procrastination. Examine that times that you find yourself procrastinating. Is it because of the task, the time of day, or your overall mood?

18. Figure out what your time is worth. If you make 30,000 a year, each hour is worth roughly $3.50 (including waking and sleeping hours). Now, decide what tasks are worth your pay and don't sweat the small stuff.

19. Set clear goals. Having a clear direction will help keep you on task. For everyone item on your

to do list, think through each step that needs to get done to complete that task.

20. Put things into perspective. Take a moment each day to take a larger picture look. This can be considering yourself in relation to your life goals, or to humanity in general.

21. Respond to email when you read it. Most people have to read an email at least twice, once when it arrives then again whenever they get around to replying to it. To cut out one reading, just reply to the email as soon as you get it.

22. Admit multitasking is bad. Studies have shown that multitasking actually inhibits productivity. The best thing to do is take on one task at a time, stay focused, and finish it before you began another task.
23. Do most important things first. Find the more urgent and vital things on your list, concrete on them first. Getting a big gorilla off your back first thing in the morning is a great way to start the day.

24. Check your email on a schedule. Find a specific time or times to check your email on a consistent basis. For example: check it first thing in the morning then right after lunch or right

before you leave for the day.

25. Keeps web site addressed organized. The fewer clicks or buttons you have to push to get to a frequented site the more time saved.

26. Know when you work your best. Some people are morning people, some afternoon, and some evening. If you work best at a certain time of the day, schedule the most urgent and vital tasks then.

27. Think about keystrokes. Use keyboard short cuts as much as possible. Changing from keyboard to mouse can slow you down. Many programs have customizable keyboard shortcuts.

28. Break large projects into smaller ones. Take a mountain and make it a molehill. By taking a larger project and making it into smaller ones you are more often reinforced for success and the tasks seem much less daunting.

29. Organize your to do list every day. Days change and so should their tasks. Every day look over your to do list and prioritize it and organize it by task type and importance. What was important the day before may not be so today.

30. Know when to take your time with a task. Rushing through a project or task can actually cost you time in the long run. Know when you need to slow down and make sure you get it right the first time.

31. Keep distractions to a minimum. Avoid the water cooler, keep the radio off, and exit the internet explorer. The more there is to distract you the more time it will take to get things done.

32. Create a to do list. It is simple and takes little time. A great opportunity to make a to do list is when your head hits the pillow at night. Keep a notepad by your bed and think through the next day or week and write down what needs to get done.

33. Reward yourself. Take time to reinforce success. Work for an hour, then a ten-minute break. When the big project gets done, a trip to the movies or theatre to unwind. This will keep you going when the going gets tough.

34. Create work/home boundaries. For the most part the rule of thumb is to leave work stuff at work and home stuff at home. Keep your home a place of rest and relaxation away from work.

35. Rest. This means sleeping well at night, getting enough sleep, and taking breaks during the day. Take walk during work and get some fresh air. Get a glass of water mid-afternoon (it will also help ease that tension headache as well). Self-care is vital to productivity.

36. Eat well. A good breakfast will ensure you stay alert for the morning time. A light lunch filled with fruits and veggies won't weigh you down and will keep you motivated through the afternoon. It is hard to concentrate when the stomach is not satisfied.

37. Get an accountability partner. Share with a co-worker the tasks that you need to get done and when they need to get done. Ask them to check in for progress periodically.

38. Forgo perfectionism. There are some tasks that require perfection, but most tasks just require that they get done. Know your job and know which ones can just be completed.

39.Complete unpleasant tasks first. Get through the muck and mud first. Take on the task you are dreading first and get it out of the way. You will be glad you did.

40. Visualize your long-term success. Do not get caught up in the small things. All the things you need to get done are in service to your long-term success and goals.

41. Create a routine. A routine is the best way to pump out consistent productivity. Find a time each day to file, check email, take breaks etc. Do it every day. The control you exercise over your day will translate into control over your to do list as well.

42. Separate to do list into priorities A, B, C. An "A" means that it has to get done, a "B" means that it should be done and a "C" means that it would be nice if it got done. Tackle A's first then work down the list.

43. Plan for emergencies. Plan ahead if you need to make a million copies or have to get a project to the other store. Traffic and copy machine meltdowns are classic and common. Plan ahead, plan extra time, and save yourself a lot of stress and heartache later on.

44. Check off items as you go. Keep track of your daily success. Checking things off your list will keep you motivated to finish the day. It is

gratifying and energizing to see what you have gotten done during the day.

45. Keep a firm yet flexible schedule. Things happen. Schedule in some flextime, for example schedule only 45 minutes of an hour, leaving 15 minutes of flextime. This will account for the coworker that just had to tell your something or the coffee the spilt on your briefcase.
46. Exercise. Exercise actually energizes your body and protects you from illness. It also releases neurotransmitters that fight against stress and depression. Exercise really is the miracle drug.

47. Take a break during the day. Take a mid-morning break and an afternoon break. Take a walk, do some stretches, get some water and have a snack.

48. Stay focused. Keep on task. Let others know that you are working and cannot be disturbed. Keep your task list and materials organized so that other tasks that are staring at you from your desk do not distract you.

49. Know your limits. Know when you just need to shut it off for the day. When your mind is spent and your body is tired, it's time to take off

for the day. Work done when you are exhausted will most often have to be redone later.

50. Keep your daily to do list small and manageable. Keep it to 5 items or less. A massive to do list will only serve to overwhelm you. Put the most important tasks on the list and then set out to work. Do not borrow tomorrow's worries (or work).

Stop Procrastination, Now!

Do you put off your work for later, only to find your deadlines steadily creeping in? Then you, my friend, are one of the millions of people afflicted by the procrastination virus. Procrastination is the biggest reason for loss of productivity and late output. Though many would not admit it, they would benefit greatly if they start their work on time.

For many people, putting off their work for later is more habit than desire. It can be so hard to get into a groove where starting your tasks in a timely fashion is a priority; especially if the consequences for being late are things that one can probably bear. If you are one of these people, yet you desire to shake off your propensity for procrastination, then you have come to the right place. Here are a few tips to help you overcome this dilemma and become a more productive and reliable person.

1. Set schedules – It is very important that you have a list of activities to accomplish per day. This will help you realistically budget your time and resources. One of the cardinal sins people commit in regards to performing their tasks is to put off their work because they feel like there is so much time left. A journal, organizer, or calendar of events will help you plan and schedule your task so that you can start them promptly and finish them on time.

2. Save the Vacation for Later – Many people put their work off for later saying, "I'll just have a little fun then buckle down to work later." While it may be true that they may have more than enough time to accomplish their tasks, it would be better if they finished their work first and relax afterwards. Wouldn't relaxation be sweeter if it were after a taxing job? If you choose to lay back and relax before doing your tasks, you will be more prone to burnout and will have nothing exciting left to look forward to after accomplishing a task. It is always better to have slack period AFTER a job than before one,

especially considering that people are wont to overusing their slack time. This is suicide if you are heading towards a deadline.

3. Never Underestimate Your Tasks – Sometimes procrastination sets in because people underestimate the resources, difficulty, and time spent for a particular task. They will usually say, "It's just mowing the lawn, it's easy; I could do it in a jiffy." The problem is, no matter how trivial the task, it still takes time and resources to accomplish. If you underestimate a task, you will most likely set too little time to do it and schedule it too close to its deadline.

4. Don't Allow Yourself to Get Comfortable Doing Nothing – It would definitely help if you kept a subconscious alarm whenever you are doing nothing. Get this alarm to remind you of things that may need to be done. This will help you foster the notion that jobs accomplished now means more time for relaxation later. However, even if this is the case, do not forget to put ample time in for rest and to remove all thoughts of troubles before hitting the sack. The trick here, however, is not to overdo you rest. There is a difference between resting and idling. Always set the right amount of time for rest and stick to that schedule.

Learn To Set Goals

There are those who are bounded by laws and rules, yet success is too distant for them. On the other hand, there are those who appears to be easy going people but are successful. Think you have what it takes to be like them? Or would you rather do something different to achieve the elusive success? Take heart and set your goals.

What do goals represent by the way? These are actually representations of your visions about you and your future. Goals should be achievable and realistic. These kinds of goals allow you to put them into practice or at least do some activities that allow you to monitor your progress. However, more is involved in just merely setting realistic goals.

Remember that in order to achieve your goals, you must act according to your goals. Otherwise, all else would be vanity if you do not exert effort in reaching them. The following will help you set achievable goals:

1. Enhance your skills in achieving targeted goals by setting objectives, as well as standard and

optional activities that will help you meet your goals.

2. Strategize and take risks in meeting your goals. Strategic thinking is very important because this will allow you to be productive and focus on the activities according to your goals.

3. Act in accordance to your goals. Proper mind setting is very important in achieving your goals.

Take the extra mile. Try taking risks but never compromise your safety. Taking risks means that you are ready to learn new things and challenges that will help you in the long run.

On one hand, you may wonder why there is a need for you to set goals if you think you have not failed at all in your endeavors. Remember that setting goals does not mean that you always fail. Setting goals means that you are acknowledging your limitations and you are ready to work your way up towards success, professionally or personally. It is for this reason why objective goals matter.

Moving forward, you also have to consider that there are goals that are just too hard to achieve on your own. At times, these goals even create conflicts that you might think of surrendering in the long run. Take heart. Everybody have similar concerns at times. If this situation occurs and you think that surrendering is the last option, why not look for a partner, a friend maybe who is willing to help you out with your goals? Collaborate with your prospective partner and learn to prioritize. If it requires spending time in plotting all the possibilities, both the pros and cons, try it.

Remember that goal setting is focused on your benefits. So try working things out and focus, focus, and focus. Minimize or avoid distractions if possible so you can work your goals better. Work that proper mindset for a clearer vision of you achieving those valuable goals. If you are vying for promotion in your workplace, it is important that you see yourself already in the position you want. If you are aiming for a personal or educational goal, make things happen by planning and doing things related to your goals. You will then realize that goals, no matter how difficult they may appear, are still valuable to consider. Once your goals are achieved, sweet success knocks on your door commending you for a job well done.

Finding Your Passion

You cannot become rich or achieve any other kind of success in life if you don't have passion about what you are doing. Be it the simplest thing or the most sophisticated thing, you need passion in order to succeed.

What's the importance of passion in your life? Where does it take you? You have a 9 to 5 job drawing a good pay, you have a good family and all's well with the world. (That's the goal hopefully, but there's even more) However, deep inside, you may feel like you are going nowhere. The job isn't moving upward either. You are actually stagnating in your career and mentally and spiritually. Something is missing.

Passion. The one quality that textbooks and instruction manuals and company procedures will never talk about, but we will discuss here. Everyone is in such a hurry to make you fit perfectly into the machine like a well-oiled gear, that they forgot you are a living, feeling human being. Even you have forgotten.

Ask yourself. If I had a million bucks in the bank, what kind of work would I be doing? Would I chuck this humdrum job and move on to something really exciting? That's something that I have always wanted to do. Then ask yourself – why am I not doing that right now? Is it because of peer pressure or because I don't want to move out of my comfort zone? Don't want to rock my boat? You are half asleep in your boat already and in a few years; you could be put out to pasture! If the boat rocks now, you could be jerked awake and come to your senses. Your passionate senses.

In the aftermath of the recession of 2008, millions of people lost their jobs. Many of them took up new vocations and suddenly found that they were finally following their dream.

Many of them are now highly successful in their newfound professions. You don't have to wait for dire straits to rock you out of your present mediocre life. You can decide right now, that you want to live and work passionately and make your life worthwhile. The Highway of Passion is an amazing ride. And Prosperity is just one of the landmarks on this route! Get ready for the ride of your life!

What's your real calling in life? So you have decided to break away from the pathetic monotony of your regular job. You want to live fully and passionately and reap all those rich rewards at the end of the rainbow. How do you find out what you are truly passionate about?

How do you separate the delusions from the do-able? You could be passionate about becoming the King of Spain, or winning the lottery or ruling the world. Indeed, there are people who have dreamt of that and done it. Alexander the Great ruled almost the entire known world in his time. But what is your true passion?

Here are a few steps you can take to discover the currents that move you deep inside:-

1. Read your own body language. How does your body behave at your present job? Does it tense up and ache all the time? Do you get panic attacks very often? Are you so bored that you doze at your desk? Do you keep looking at the clock as break time approaches? Then you are in the wrong job. You simply don't have the passion for it. When you work on a job that you are passionate about, all your aches and cramps will dissolve. You will find yourself working extra hours, talking to your friends about your work and simply bubbling with life.

2. What did you love doing as a child? Your childhood hobbies and obsessions can indicate a genuine passion. Education and family pressures often move us away from our true calling. Did you love bikes or gardening or trekking? Then maybe a career in the automobile or landscaping or travel industries is where you should be! So sit back and recall your childhood and write down your memories. What made you smile then may still make you grin today and in the future.

3. What do you love doing as an adult? You might very well have passionate side pursuits even today. Do you love your moonlighting job more than your regular day job? Many corporate honchos work the night shift as chefs or night school teachers. Start spending a few hours every day on your pet hobby. It may just hold the key to the real you!

Sometimes to unleash true passion in yourself, you may have to change your job to suit your aptitude better. But you may find that you do love your existing job, but simply don't feel very passionate about it. You can study your situation and then try to make a few changes to rekindle the passion you felt when you first started working. Visualize yourself working passionately at your job. What would you be feeling? A sharp focus, clear vision of your future, total control and mastery over your work, a healthy body and an exuberant attitude! Then reverse engineer these symptoms to regain your passion.

Check on whether you work better with a team on the field rather than those solitary hours at a desk. Are you logical minded or creative minded? Are you crunching numbers when you would rather be in the design section? Get a revised aptitude assessment done. Ask your superior for a transfer to a more appropriate department. Exercise your body for at least thirty minutes every day. Let the adrenaline pump and flow in your blood. Eat healthy food and drink a lot of water. Quit smoking and using any stimulants. Restore the balance between your spirituality and physicality by meditation and prayer. Your refreshed body will invigorate your mind and passion will return.

Increase your knowledge of your field by taking new study courses. Take time out to travel and widen your perspective. Take a half-pay sabbatical to add new qualifications to your resume. Some lateral career movement can bring an innovative twist in your way of working.

Passion does not come overnight. Taking these proactive steps will see a gradual increase in your enthusiasm. You will begin working with a newly fired zeal, which becomes contagious, motivating your teammates as well. You will have consciously taken charge of your life again and the fruits of prosperity will be in sight once again.

When you are young, your motivation for working and living lies in larger income, better standards of living and in general having a good time. But as you grow older, your priorities change. You want something more fulfilling. You seek to achieve goals that you will be remembered for. A sense of urgency begins to set in as time passes. And the source of your passion arises from wanting to leave behind a legacy. That legacy may take the form of social change brought about by your work. Or it can be in an enterprise or institution founded by you. Many successful businessmen set up foundations and trusts in the pursuit of noble causes. Thus they seek to perpetuate their name or family name for posterity. An invention or a new process or a novel product can also enshrine the maker's name in the books of history.

Temporal pleasures and petty rewards do not satisfy someone working at this level. His or her passion seeks loftier goals. The greater the goal, the more fervent the passion. Revolutionaries and freedom fighters like Malcolm X and Dr. Martin Luther King struggled most all their lives for the liberation of their people. Their ambitions encompassed the lives of millions of their people. The sheer magnitude of their legacy consumed their entire lifetime, but it was a passionate lifetime, with every day spent in pursuit of that goal. How do you set about leaving behind your legacy? What is it that you feel strongly about? Write down your strongest emotions and issues. They may even lie outside your present work area. Start working on those issues. Educate yourself and acquire new skills if you have to, and get to work. It may be a simple project like improving your community, or a major reform of state laws. Remember that all the great men and women who have brought about change were ordinary men like you and me, but they had the power of conviction and passionate belief in their dreams.

In modern sports we see the same phenomenon displayed with players and their coaches. A dynamic coach can inspire his team to put in a passionate performance. If the players do not have faith in the coach or their fellow teammates, the team fails to coordinate and the game is lost.

The faith equation between sportsman and trainer is particularly important in endurance sports like gymnastics and athletics. A footballer may in turn be driven by his faith in his fans. A corporate executive may be passionate about his employees and shareholders. Faith, emotion and inspiration are alive and kicking in every corner of human activity.

Which external agency are you focusing on? God? Your boss? Your coach? Your community or country? Decide on what moves you and use that agency as a star to guide you and drive your passion. Getting passionate about your career and blazing a glorious path at the office is great. But don't let your loved ones suffer from a lack of passion at home. A proper balance has to be struck by giving love to your significant other and children too. A passionate lifelong affair with your significant other can do wonders in your work life too. You are happy and relaxed and your body glows with the healing effects of healthy loving sex. The love you shower on your children is also reciprocated many times over.

A man is truly respected if he excels in all his roles – as a worker, a son, a husband and a father (and even a grandfather) and a community member. Devote time and passion to all these roles. When you have genuinely mastered the art of passion, you will find that it pervades every minute of your day, be it in the boardroom or bedroom or playroom. Passion can become a double-edged sword if not wielded properly. Spending hours and hours of obsessed extra time at the workplace can affect your health as well as your family relations. Neglecting to attend your son's school events and not cheering him at his football match can create an alienation that can never be repaired. An unfulfilled spouse can also prove very damaging in the long run. A marriage can fall apart and a string of unhappy one-night stands can never take the place of a loving caring relationship. Passion is not about throwing huge family parties where everyone can feed on your wealth. It isn't about giving a no limit credit card to your wife or the latest bike to your son. It is spending time and effort to share your life and soul with your loved ones. Passion lies in transmitting your passion for life to your children, your wife and all around you.

How has my fathering been affected by what I learned about being a father?

_____

_____

_____

_____

_____

_____

What did I learn about character from my father (or father figure)? What did I learn that was good? What did I learn that was not so good?

_____

_____

_____

_____

_____

What did I learn about character from my mother (or mother figure)? What did I learn that was good? What did I learn that was not so good?

_____

_____

_____

_____

_____

_____

Which traits in my character have served me well
as a father? How will I continue to use these traits
to raise healthy children?

_____

_____

_____

_____

_____

_____

_____

How will I show my children that I have good character?

_____

_____

_____

_____

_____

_____

Which fathering skills am I really good at?

_____

_____

_____

_____

_____

_____

How can I build on my fathering strengths? How can I address my fathering challenges?

_____

_____

_____

_____

_____

_____

How was I raised to express or not express my emotions?

_____

_____

_____

_____

_____

_____

Which feelings and emotions do I express? Which ones do I suppress?

_____

_____

_____

_____

_____

_____

Am I a good model to my children of a man who is in touch with his emotions and who appropriately expresses them? If not, what do I need to do to become a better model?

_____

_____

_____

_____

100+ Daily Activities And Mindsets Challenges

The purpose of these challenges is simple. I want you to think differently everyday. Depending on how you operate on a daily basis, you may have a set of routines that you do, and may feel like you are not getting the most of your day. Or even your life. The following are simple and easy things you can do to make your life a little more interesting, a little more exciting and a little more meaningful. Here's the 100+ daily challenges, I challenge you to share this list with someone you think could use a little more in their life. Okay, let's go.

1. Apologize to someone you know you have wronged.

2. Eat 100% healthy for the whole day.

3. Write, not type a letter and send it to someone.

4. Start that hobby you have been meaning to start.

5. Dress up for not special occasion.

6. Spend the day outside, the worse the conditions, the better.

7. Mediate for ten minutes, music optional.
8. Attend a different church with a friend.

9. Listen to some old school music while enjoying some old photos.

10. Do some volunteer work.

11. Read book in its entirety.

12. Go for a long walk without music, just your thoughts.

13. Enjoy your favorite meal with someone and take your time.

14. Buy ten items from the Dollar Store and give each item to ten different individuals.

15. Make eye contact with each stranger you come across.

16. Go a day with your phone or computer/laptop.

17. Reward yourself for having a great day.

18. Give thanks to the Lord. Say it out loud.

19. Make a plan on how you will rid yourself of a bad habit that you have.

20. Workout within the first five minutes of waking up.

21. List 5 things you want to accomplish this week.

22. Visualize your ideal career, then ask yourself why you are not doing it.

23. For each meal eat something you have never tried before.

24. Look over you finances and see where you will be in the next 5, 10 and 20 years.

25. Call someone you haven't talked to in awhile.

26. Clean your closet and donate a bag of clothes you don't wear.

27. Review your offline and online friends and make much needed deletions.

28. Back up your laptop/computer on an external hard drive.

29. Give a gift to a random friend.

30. Drive a new route to work.

31. Wake up and declare that you will be focused and positive today.

32. Write a blog and find somewhere to share it.

33. Donate at least five dollars to charity.

34. Assist a friend in a goal you know they are trying to reach.

35. Make a couple sack lunches for the homeless.

36. Buy a Megaball lottery ticket and make the drawing an event at your house.

37. Write out 10 accomplishments in your life.

38. Watch some Ted Talks on YouTube.

39. Greet everyone with a hello and a smile.

40. Think about how you can help a total stranger.

41. Learn a couple of words in a new language.

42. Apply for your dream job, even if you are not qualified.

43. Go out of town nearby and sightsee.

44. Think about starting a business. If you already do, think about how you can take it to the next level

45. Call a close relative.

46. Tell someone a secret about yourself.

47. Kick it with a friend.

48. Write down something that's been bothering you. Decide to handle it or burn the paper along with you stressing over it again.

49. Focus on one agenda today.

50. Go to indie band show.

51. Tell someone you love that you love him or her.

52. Sing to someone.

53. Do a pushup challenge with a friend or by yourself.

54. Fantasize on your dream overseas vacation. Then, write out the details to make it happen.

55. Kick back and relax to your favorite album.

56. Engage in a conversation with a stranger.

57. Become an avid for a cause.

58. 100% honesty, no small white lies.

59. Get a photo with a celebrity.

60. Hang out at a coffee shop.

61. Collaborate with someone on a mutual interest.
62. Spend day watching movies.

63. No multi-tasking all day.

64. Shop small business.

65. Ask yourself if you are being the best you.

66. Learn something about a subject matter you are interested in.

67. List your positive qualities.

68. Ask that special person out on a date.

69. Donate blood.

70. List your fears and conquer at least one of them.

71. Donate something to the military.

72. Thank someone from your past.

73. Pick up litter in your neighborhood.

74. Have a high intensity workout.

75. Challenge someone to be better.

76. Take a calculated risk in business or personal life.

77. Discuss your passions with someone.

78. Read about a subject matter you don't care about.

79. Run Forest Run.

80. Pay it forward at a local business.

81. Look at the positive in negative situations.

82. Compliment a stranger.

83. Do something for your neighbor.

84. Make a video and post it online.

85. Instead of buying it, make it.

86. Write a song and give it to a local musician.

87. Write a short book. It's possible because you are reading one now.

88. Make a playlist and listen to it while you drive around your city.

89. Watch a movie you have never heard of.

90. Go to the library.

91. Attend a free event.

92. Start a conversation with a homeless person.

93. Cook something you have cooked before.

94. Write a poem for someone.

95. Make a to do list and complete it.

96. Walk into an ice cream shop, buy ice cream for the next person in line and walk out.

97. No fast food.

98. Write a short letter to yourself and view it in exactly one year.

99. Join a local club or community.

100. Eliminate clutter in your house.

101. Buy a new outfit.

102. Say no when that's how you feel.

103. Meet and introduce yourself to someone that's in the industry you are in.

104. Do something today that you were going to do tomorrow or later.

105. Take pictures and develop them.

106. Leave positive post it notes around town.

107. No television.

108. Do something you always wanted to do

109. Hug ten people.

110. Do something that scares you.

111. Forgive someone you are upset with.

Obviously you don't have to do each of these daily, but challenging yourself to complete some of these activities will keep each day fresh and engaging.

Stay Focused

Things To Keep In Mind

Discharge planning is a formal process that begins 60 days before an inmate discharges to make arrangements for basic necessities. A counselor will meet with the inmate to discuss the following items. Such as medication, housing, employment, identification reentry programs and more.

A family member or friend can pick up an inmate directly at the facility on the day of their discharge. If a ride is not available, transportation can be provided to the facility closet to your home address. You must notify your counselor in advance to make arrangements.

Be an expert of your child's development. Children go through a lot of developmental stages before they reach adulthood and you have to stay in the 'know', so you know. Use resources available to you to understand what is going in the world around your child and ask questions to stay abreast on how they are handling things.

Just because you are in prison or not living with your child, doesn't mean you can be their

biggest supporter. Whatever your child is interested, learn all you can about it, so you can engage them in conversation about it or give them pointers.

Participate in any parenting programs that are available to you. In addition, read different parenting books, not just the fatherhood ones. Read motherhood books as well. You will be surprise at what mothers endure along the way in their motherhood journey. It also will make you a well-rounded parent.

Mentioned earlier but can't be mentioned enough. Make sure your child knows that they are not responsible for your incarceration. Reassure them that they did nothing wrong and you wish you could be with them but you have to do your time first.

Encourage your child to be a child. In today's world, children are growing up to fast in sense of knowing adult matters and participating in those adult situations. Children should not have to deal with the burdens of adults. Urge them to play, learn and grow as a child.

Remember you can't tell your child you love them enough. Write with love, talk with love

and show them love. A child that knows that they have unconditional love will display more confident, self worth and healthy behavioral habits.

Be honest and humble with your children. If you want to create a trust-worthy bond with your children they must know that they can trust and believe in what you say and do. They also need to know that they can come to you with anything and not be judged but supported.

Show respect to others, especially the parental guardian. Be the model you want your children to follow.

Pray with and for your children. Develop a relationship with Jesus Christ. You will never feel alone if you do so. Allow the Spirit to guide you. Encourage your children to follow a spiritual path.

Take care of your health, mentally and physically. Exercise and read every day. Living a healthy lifestyle will keep you around longer to enjoy life and your family.

Call, write and have your child visit as often as possible. Make contacting your child constant and consistent. If you develop a routine for contacting, stick to it. Make a commitment to yourself and your child that you know you can maintain.

Take advance of any job training that is available to you. That includes computer classes. It's not about what you are interested in; it's about making yourself more valuable to potential employers. Upon your release, make the local employment office your second home.

Be sure to have a valid driver's license or ID. Get together all the paperwork you will eventually need such as birth certificate, resume, etc.

Get educated while you away. If your institution offers GED classes or college work, take advantage of it. This will go a long way towards bettering yourself for the workforce.

When you get a job, pay what you owe. Whether it's child support or restitution, make arrangements to pay. Don't work hard to get your fresh start and allow something like child support sends you right back.

Find a support group to keep you motivated and guide you in the right direction. Search them out

before you are released so you can connect with them as soon as you are out.

Know where you want to be in your life in the next month, next year. Make a plan to reaching that goal. Be honest and realistic in making this plan. Work at this plan everyday. Every thing you do should move you closer to achieving your ultimate goal.

Be patient with your Fresh Start process. It's not going to be easy but it is necessary you remain patient and positive about the process. Adjustments will be needed to be made and time will have to pass before some things can be put in place. Once again, be patient.

Forgive others as well as yourself if it is necessary for you move on and begin your fresh start. Dwelling in the past won't move you forward. Acknowledge and move on. A lot of time and energy goes into living in the past, and that time and energy that can be used towards your Fresh Start. You can say you are sorry and ask for forgiveness but your actions will show if you mean it or not.

If you make the commitment towards a Fresh Start, do it. This means "No" to the following:

No playing the victim

No breaking promises

No returning to your old ways

No doubting yourself

No avoiding your problems

No ducking responsibilities

No messing with people's emotions

No negative thoughts and actions

Say "Yes" to everything that is Family First.

Getting Work

Before you read this chapter, check your mindset. Some of the things you read in this chapter may seem generic, boring, unattainable and wishful thinking, but with a positive and can do attitude, you can make it happen.

Also, you can't focus on what people are going to think about you being an ex-con. Your focus should be on attaining employment, improving yourself/relationships and performing your daddy duties. You will be denied for jobs because of your past. You will be pushed away because of your past. People will avoid you because of your past. However, you have to remain focused on your objectives and move forward.

Here is a list of companies that hire ex-convicts. Life after prison is difficult and getting a job after prison can be really tough. I pray that you find success in properly contacting these companies and securing employment. Make sure you are ready to work before contacting them, i.e. your resume, your contact information, reliable transportation, and the willingness to do the very best you can at whatever position you receive. Visit the companies' website to get contact information, locations and application procedures.

The List:

AAMCO Transmissions
Abbott Laboratories
Ace Hardware
Alamo Rent a Car
Alberto-Culver
Allied Van Lines
Allstate Insurance Company
America West Airlines
American Express
American Greetings
Aon
Apple
Archer Daniels Midland
ARCO
Arthur J. Gallagher & Co.
Atlas Van Lines
Avis Rent a Car System
Avon Products
Bally Technologies
Baskin Robbins
Baxter International
Best Foods
Best Western

BFGoodrich Aerospace
Black & Decker
Blue Cross Blue Shield Association
Boeing
Bridgestone
British Airways
Brunswick Corporation
Budget Rent a Car
Campbell Soup Company
Canon Inc.
Career Education Corporation
Carrier Corporation
Casio
Caterpillar Inc.
CDW
Chase
Chicago Mercantile Exchange
Cintas
Coes-Coin
Coldwell Banker
Compaq
ConAgra Foods
Dairy Queen
DAP Products
Deer Park Spring Water
Del Monte Foods
Delta Air Lines
Delta Faucet Company
Denny's

Dole Food Company
Dollar Rent A Car
Dow Jones & Company
Dunkin' Donuts
Dunlop Tires
DuPont
Duracell
Equity Office
Exelon
Exxon Mobil
Federal Express
Firestone Tire and Rubber Company
First Health Group Corporation
Fortune Brands
Fruit of the Loom
Fujifilm
General Electric
General Growth Properties
General Mills
Georgia-Pacific
GMAC Real Estate
Hanes
Aon Hewitt
Hilton Hotels & Resorts
Illinois Tool Works
Kmart
Kraft Foods
L.A. Times
Mobil Oil

Molex
Motorola
Navistar International
Newsweek Inc.
Niki
Nisource
Northern Trust
Old Republic International
Packaging Corporation of America
Pactiv
Pepsi
Philip Morris Companies Inc.
RR Donnelly
Newell Rubbermaid
Sara Lee Corporation
Sears
ServiceMaster
Dr Pepper/Seven Up
Shell Oil Company
Showtime Networks
Smurfit-Stone Container
Sony Corporation
Air Southwest
Sprint Corporation
Target
Telephone and Data Systems
Tellabs
Tribune Media
U.S. Cellular

Uneven Investments
United Airlines
Verizon Communications
W.W. Grainger
Walgreens
Walmart
William Wrigley Jr. Company
Yard House
Zebra Technologies
Zenith Electronics
Xerox

You may be saying to yourself, 'I haven't even heard of some of these companies' or 'I don't stand a chance at getting hired at these companies'. You cannot have that self -doubting attitude and eliminate yourself from jobs you haven't even looked into or applied. This list should instill an optimistic mindset and hope for the future. Check to see which of these companies have offices local to you. Don't forget to use employment sources such as the department of labor in your city, online sites such as Monster, Indeed and Careerbuilder, the classifieds, and ask around your family and friends. Remember, securing employment is just as important as maintaining your relationships. Until you are working full time, looking for employment will need to be full time.

There are plenty of other side hustles you can research and create. To assist you with your job hunting and possibly starting your own, take advantage of the vocational education courses possibly available where you are incarcerated. Some prisons offer auto body technology, building maintenance, carpentry, computer repair, small engine repair and more. This course could serve you well on the outside.

Library services are available in most facilities. Books are available as well as some limited legal resource information.

Explaining a Conviction on Your Resume

No matter what resources you utilize, you will probably have to fill out an application. Since most companies will do a background check on you, it is important to tell the truth on the form. Here are some things to consider:

- Read the question carefully and only give them what they ask for. Make sure you don't offer information that they did not request.

- Do your own background check. If you know what will appear on the employer's check, you will be better prepared to address it.

- Be specific about what happened but do not use that time to plead innocence or deny that you did something.

- Be positive. Make sure you tell the employer about the positive experiences and job experience that you have had and how you have moved forward.

Starting Your Own Business

Securing employment isn't necessarily the only route to start receiving an income. You can start your own business or at least a side hustle (legal) until you can lock down steady employment.

Below you will find a list of side hustles you can do with little money or resources. Hopefully, you can use several of these side hustles or at least one immediately. Even if you feel you are not am to execute any of these, use them to develop your own concept for a side hustle.

However, if you have a support system in place, you will have the resources to begin some of these side hustles. If you are reading this while still incarcerated, start formulating how you will be able to create some of these side hustles by soliciting your friends and family members for the supplies and potential clientele.

They won't all work for you, but something on this list is will get you going. Taking action on something is a great way of figuring out what concept is best for you.

And now the list...

Driver Service. If you have a nice a car or SUV, ridesharing can work for you. You can earn some cash driving people around. Check out www.Lyft.com, Uber.com or other driving services to see how you can get in on this opportunity.

Car Detailing. You can start with hooking up your neighbors or meeting clients at their house to clean their vehicles. If you are able to get a portable tank of water, then you can start taking on clients at their office, malls, schools or even attracting potential clients at parking lots.

Baker/Personal Chef. If you have a niche for cooking, then personal chef or baker is for you. Provide cakes, chicken, cookies or other culinary delights for corporate events, parties and friends.

Website/App Developer. If you are tech savvy

and have a nice computer, then you can get in on the ever-growing tech industry. Startup companies and entrepreneurs can use someone to take care of the technological aspects of running a business so they can focus on everything. There are get sites to help you along in the development of the sites and apps for your clients.

Personal Trainer/Boot Camp Instructor.

People want to get in shape, lots of people. You can hold classes outside in parking lots or at parks and it cost you nothing. Or you can find clients and use the same gym they have a membership at and work out of there.

Tutor. Math, Science or English, if you excel in these subjects or others, you can earn money tutoring. Stop by your local school district office or college campuses to find potential students. You can easily earn $25 or more an hour.

Moving/Hauling Service. If you have a truck, then every weekend or end of the month, someone is going to need moving services. You can network apartment and real estate companies to be the official hauler and mover for their properties.

Painter. You can partner with a professional painter to get some extra tips if you're not sure how to charge. Once again, network with apartment and real estate companies.

House Cleaner. As with the moving service and painter gigs, partnering with real estate agents and apartment properties for leads helps. Develop what your niche as far as cleaning is and that's how you will grab clients. Your friends and neighbors are an option as well.

Run Errands/Personal Assistant. You know people in your own circle who're just too busy with work and their family. Trust me; there are thousands more in your city that can use someone to run their errands. Services you can provide can include grocery shopping, walking dogs, picking up their kids, and picking up supplies for their business.

Handy Man. If you have the skills, let it be known to everyone you known. Whether its repairing household appliances, doors, walls, painting or whatever your skill set is; there's a need.

Photographer. If you have a nice camera and

have skills in photoshopping, then look into becoming a photographer. Decide on your niche and specialize in those types of photos i.e. weddings, parties, musicians, etc....

Freelance Writer. Network with bloggers to get a guest post feature on their sites or look up freelance websites for gigs that are available. If you been on sites that look like they can use some assistance, reach out to them.

Accounting Services. If you have a good understanding in accounting then you can go to small businesses and individuals and assist them with their bookkeeping. Tax season is an excellent time to get the word out about your services.

Lawn Service. With a lawnmower and a couple of other lawn tools, you can go into the lawn service business. Your neighborhood is a great place to start.

Internet Researcher. Your ability to navigate the Internet can make you money. Students, small businesses and entrepreneurs can really use this service.

Social Media Guru. Musicians, entrepreneurs, bloggers and other small businesses can use the services of someone that knows the in's and out's of social media. Creating their social media presence, updating and responding to their fans and clients is what will be required of you.

Virtual Administrative Assistant. If you have experience and/or knowledge in applications such as Internet Research Schedule Management, Manage & Sort Emails, Correspondence Documents, Word Processing, Writing/Proofreading/Editing, Distribution Database, Creation/Management, Customer Relations, Contact Management. Then you should consider becoming a V.A. Assistant. Also, you get to work from home.

Pet Walker. If you love pets, this is the side business for you. You can simply just walk their pets or add services like taking the pets to veterinarian appointments and pet sit. Fiverr.com. The Fiverr website allows you to list services you will provide starting at $5 such as logo design, proofreading, virtual assistant and much, much more. There are more than 3 millions gigs on Fiverr, so make sure you check out the competition to see how your gig can stand out. I've purchased gigs from Fiverr on multiple occasions, so I say it's the real deal.

These side hustles were just the tip of the iceberg on side hustles you can start. The following are a list of websites that allow you to get your side hustling on much like Fiverr.com. Check them out and see what works for you.

Upwork.com
Freelancer.com
Shiftgig.com
Craiglist.com
Konsus.com
Needto.com
Fancyhands.com
MechanicalTurk.com
ShortTask.com
GrowthGeeks.com
Scribendi.com
Rev.com
ServiceScape.com
Taskrabbit.com
Takl.com
Zaarly.com
Handy.com
Houzz.com
Jiffy.com
FieldAgent.co
Gigwalk.com
Bestmark.com

Get online and search what you want to do exactly for work and you will find a wide range of options. Make the plan and do the work. Good luck.

What Is Financial Empowerment?

The term financial empowerment" has many aspects. On a general note, it means being self-sufficient with money, so much so that you don't keep wanting for more. You have your financial reserves full and for any of your needs, you just have to plunge into them and get at the money. A person who is financially empowered is thus dynamic economically as well because he or she is able to use money to attract more money. Some of you who are reading this are probably looking for employment and feel this chapter isn't for you. Think again. Having a clear understanding of finances will prepare you for when you have the cash flow you desire.

Ability vs. Action

There is a wide gulf between ability and action in the world that we live in. There are millions of people out there who are capable of doing something. They might even have the right academic qualifications and some might even have the experience. But then these people aren't putting their talents to the right use. Think about something that can teach excellently, but doesn't put that talent to use. This teacher is instead doing a desk job because according to him or her that's a safer bet. Now, the desk job can only take the person so far because he or she doesn't really like doing that stuff. However, if this person had taken the bigger step of going ahead and teaching – overcoming any limitations in the way, such as stage fright – it is highly possible that he or she would be much better financially stable and empowered today. We all have various talents, but we fail to discover them and even if we do, we fail to put them to use. J. K. Rowling would not have become the multimillionaire she is today if she had given up her penchant for writing and chased a "humdrum safe" job like most of us do.

Think what Barack Obama would have been if he did not act to implement his immense leadership potential and charisma to rule one of the most developed nations of the world.

The one thing we have to consider is that it is not just enough to be able. It is not enough to be able to swim, cook, dance, write, jump or whatever. If you want to be financially empowered, you have to use these abilities that are within you and wow the people around you. It is only then that you start taking steps toward your empowerment.

The Four Fundamentals

When you are looking at building yourself financially, there are a few things that you must make sure you have with you. These are your allies in your quest for financial empowerment – they are your four fundamentals – without which you will find this journey very difficult.

Here we take at a look at these four essentials in brief and throughout this chapter, we shall take a detailed look at what they really mean.

Assets

Assets are the material and nonmaterial things that you have with you. These things are valuable because you use them to create more things. However, we are going to bring about a change in your perspective of assets. Normally people think only about monetary assets. But everything that you have, including the love of your spouse, can become an asset.

Education

Education is veritable factors in empowering yourself financially because your career is going to depend on how educated you are. However, education does not just mean academic qualifications – everything that you do in the pursuit of achieving something counts toward your education. Even reading a manual to understand how a particular software application operates will be education for you because you can use it in the future.

Investment
Investing is an asset because this helps you in securing money for the long run. When things are going the way they shouldn't, your investments matter a lot. Even when everything is hunky-dory, your investments build up your financial portfolio like few other things can.

Recreation
You might not willingly take this as a factor for financial empowerment, but the fact is that you need to enrich your mind in order to stay healthier and hence make yourself more stable monetarily. Some forms of recreation can actually directly help in improving your economic standing as well.

The Sum of Five
The Sum of Five is a key aspect in financial empowerment. It is a rule, a rule that you apply in order to keeping yourself dynamic. It ensures that you don't remain stuck in the rut when you have achieved a modicum of success, but you

keep improving upon it and keep moving northward. So, what does the Sum of Five state?

The Sum of Five states that if your income is the sum total of the five people closest to you. If the five most prominent people you are dealing with financially make less money than you do, then it is time for you to find some more financial collaborators.

This is the statement of the Sum of Five, but you need not judge it by what it actually says. Look at what it means. What it means is this – When you are involved in a business collaboration with several people, you must take a look at how much the five people closest to you are earning. Here, we don't really mean a number at all. The "five" is irrelevant. You have to look at the people you are dealing with at all times. If the people you are dealing with are making more money than you are, you must continue your efforts till you reach their level. But if they are all making less money than you, it means you have reached a point of stagnancy and now you need to find more people to associate with.

You won't be mistaken if you find this law to be a bit selfish. Actually, it isn't that way. We all believe and accept that change is imminent. We say that all the time. Then why do we not change the circumstances that surround us? We tend to live in the same situation for life, without trying to think we should take higher leaps. This is where we make the absolute error.

If we want to progress, it is important for us to improve the situation that we are surrounded with. It is important for us to change the set of people we regularly deal with. There is a saying in an Indian language that says, "A man doesn't really succeed in life unless he leaves his childhood behind." What it really means is that we should not cling to our past more than we should.

In life, we continue climbing the rungs of ladder of success but since we tend to think we have reached our peak, we never continue moving upward. This is when the downward fall begins.

Understanding the Concept of Assets

Assets are what you utilize in order to start empowering yourself financially. These assets include monetary as well as monetary resources. Most people only consider monetary assets when they speak about assets. They consider things like their bank balance, their property, their cars, their stocks, etc. as assets. However, there is much more to assets than just these materialistic things.

Here we take a look at assets other than the usual material ones.

Goodwill
Your good name in the market is a veritable asset. It could be your name or the name of your company, your brand, etc. Whatever goodwill your name has accumulated, you could certainly use it in improving your profits, and hence it becomes an asset. For instance, if you launch a new product with the same name of your previous successful product, it already gets a lot of foundation to succeed. That's the reason big name companies sell their goodwill when they give out franchises.

Your Qualifications, Eligibilities and Experiences
Everything that you do in your life is an asset in itself. These are things you can tap on in order to empower yourself in a better manner. For example, if you are a postgraduate, you could use that qualification to pitch in for financing a research plant you want to set up. If you have worked in a particular area, your chances of earning in that area are more.

Your Family, Friends and Other People

Everyone that you come in contact with is a potential asset for you. You are what your family makes you, and that decides your capabilities to a large extent. Also, your friends make you and so do other people that you come in contact with. People are so important to businesses today that there are complete business models that are set up on this concept. Take network marketing, for instance, better known as MLM, where people directly tap into the people they know in order to enhance their income capabilities.

Building Your Assets

Being financially empowered means you have to have enough money so that you don't lack for funds when you need them. You have to be rich enough to have money to cover all your needs and desires. The desires part needs to be seen with more careful attention here, because most people have adequate money to cover their needs. It is when they need to realize one of their dreams that they feel they are lacking in proper funds.

It is necessary that you have the right kind of financial empowerment to chase your goals and intentions. This is where asset building becomes important in your route to financial empowerment. In this context, you try to build on what you can call your own so that you can build more to call your own. There are various ways in which you can begin focusing on asset building.

Proper Investments
Investing is the best route to building assets. Find ways to make investments, such as in fixed deposits in banks, money back insurance policies, stocks or whatever suits your interests.
The channel you select for investment should be safe and should guarantee you high returns.

Sniffing Out Opportunities
Opportunities are all around us, but we don't know how to get at them. Keep your eyes wide open. If there is a business venture that interests you, learn more about it till you know all that there is to it. There are several high-paying opportunities like network marketing that can pay you back a lot without requiring much investment. Keep your mind receptive to such opportunities.

Involve Your Friends and Family
Most of us shut out our near and dear ones when it comes to asset building. We have to understand that assets are not just monetary. There are various other things that can help us build

ourselves financially, and toward this end, we have to realize that the role of the people in our lives is quite significant.

Investing in Education for Your Financial

What we don't really realize is that our encounter with financial empowerment begins much sooner than we think. It isn't when we are 20 and thinking about a career; it is right when we are 3 and attend our first school. In fact, our financial empowerment begins even before that when our parents lovingly and patiently tell us what is what. All those questions, all those attempts at gathering information and, later, education, are nothing but steps toward financially empowering ourselves.

For, what is education if not a way to empower ourselves in every way, including financially?

A lot of people tap into their educational qualifications when they are looking for a job, pitching for a promotion, applying for a freelancing assignment or even when applying for financial assistance for a commercial venture. The educational qualification is a kind of abstract collateral; it is something people judge your financial worth with. If you are better qualified they know that you will keep sailing through and hence they don't mind extending a better financial help for your ventures. They don't mind investing in your ventures either because they consider you as a worthy candidate with their money. That is the reason, it is important to learn as much as possible.

After becoming the President of the United States, one of the first things Barack Obama did was to give a clarion call to his people to go back to school. This does not really mean physically going back to school, but it means continuing to learn something or the other as we did when we were younger.

Come to think of it, when we were at school, we would learn a new thing each day. Are we doing that right now? At school, we enriched our minds each day and became what we are today. But why has this process of becoming stopped for some people? Why do some people think that their learning age has ceased? We need to educate ourselves continuously, till the last day of our lives and keep improving ourselves.

When we are more educated, we not only learn better avenues to earn money but we also learn how to manage the money properly so that it keeps growing. No form of education should be intimidating and there is no age when you cannot begin learning something.

Enriching Your Financial Reserves with Recreation

The common mentality of most people is that when they are getting some recreation for themselves – in whatever form that might be – they are actually wasting time. They think that by giving themselves some amusement, they are actually depriving themselves of the opportunity of being able to earn something. Proverbs like "Wasting time is akin to wasting money" don't help matters one bit. But we should remember, "All work and no play make Jack a dull boy." But, is it only a dull boy that Jack can turn out to be? No, worse things can happen if you deprive yourself from proper routes of recreation. You have to understand what recreation means first. To recreate means to free up your mind and utilize it in doing something that you really like to do. It means to unwind yourself from your daily rigmarole of work. Since our mind is not a machine, but a living organ with blood and tissues in it, it does need this kind of unwinding ourselves.

But there is a subtle point that you must understand. Every person chooses his or her form of recreation and this is most times connected with what they do professionally. For example, for a person who teaches, reading could be a form

of recreation. Now, this is actually helping their profession in
various ways. This person is able to expand his or her knowledge and that really helps them in their profession. For a professional sportsperson, looking at someone else's game could be recreation. Now, they could pick up various tips from that and learn.

However, even when you think there are no obvious benefits of your form of recreation on your profession, there are actually several benefits. Consider that you have a desk job.
Your mode of recreation is to shoot villains in computer games. How does this help your profession? It actually does, in a very poignant way, because it helps clear the clutter of monotony that your job has created and gives you a chance to do something that revitalizes your energy. You are refreshed and can even return to work the next day in a better mood.
Remember that empowering yourself financially does not mean immersing yourself in money-related thoughts and keeping yourself there all the time. Sometimes, you have to come out of those shackles and think in a liberated manner.
This helps you rethink things and you begin looking at the world with a renewed perspective.

The Long Haul

It may not sound pleasant to a lot of us, but when most of us think of the term "financial empowerment", they tend to think about short-term goals. They think about how they can put in efforts to achieve money in the short term, within just a few weeks probably. One of the biggest mistakes that we do is that we contract our entire lifespan into a few weeks by thinking in this manner. We forget that we have a long life ahead of us and that if you want to be really financially empowered, we have to make sure that we have enough for that period which looms ahead of us.

That is why, when we speak about financial empowerment, it is not going to be much about what you can do that can give you returns today – there is a lot of material on that already – but it is about what you can do so that you stay financially empowered for the longer term. This is actually what must interest each and every one of us. There are some very important ways in which this can be done.

Education

Now, everyone gets basic education and hence if you want to really financially empower yourself, you have to learn something more than the other person. We aren't talking about childhood education here but education that enriches you as a professional. In the Internet marketing environment, for example, a person who has educated himself or herself to use blogs and article submissions will do better than someone who uses just article submissions.

Investing
People who are in for the long haul will always think closely about investment options. They will think where they can invest so that they can get the best returns. Investment is highly important if you want to financially empower yourself because this is what can help you when the chips are down.

Insurance
Insurance is an assurance that is of value when something goes horribly wrong. There are several unforeseen things that can happen in our lives; one such stroke can wipe out all the financial empowerment that we have achieved for ourselves. Though any loss in the world can never be replenished completely, insurances do provide some respite in such events.

Recreation
Every song you hear, every book you read, every movie you watch, and every place you visit

enriches your mind in some way. Though you aren't doing these things for gaining knowledge, they are certainly expanding what you know. You are learning new things and anything can be important at any time. Hence, even the way you amuse your mind is essential when you are talking about financial empowerment. All these things won't bring money right away at your doorstep, but they are definitely enhancing your capabilities. You become a better person, financially and otherwise, when you use these key factors in the right way.

Staying Upwardly Mobile
Our finishing touch will be to speak about how you must remain always moving toward the top. In fact, we have alluded to this already when we spoke about the Sum of Five. When you try to equate yourself with your collaborators and then find better collaborators if you find they are all doing much worse than you, you are staying upwardly mobile. When you mix around with people who have a particular kind of status, it automatically begins rubbing on you. Consciously or subconsciously, you begin taking steps to be with them, and sooner than you think, you are there. You get that one important breakthrough and you get to be with these people. If you have used the four fundamentals in

the right way, and are still constantly using them, then you will keep shaping yourself to be a more significant person financially. You will be going upward all the time and this is what really matters. One thing that you have to keep in mind is that you must broaden your approaches. Once you are set with something, move on to other things. We have spoken about how you must be always aware of opportunities and take them in your stride.

Learn how to make the most of them.

Think positive. Think big. When you do that, you usually do big. If you confine yourself to thinking narrow-mindedly, you are going to stay there. A lot of modern philosophers have laid great emphasis on the importance of thought – Stephen Covey, Rhonda Byrne, Paulo Coelho – and you have to understand that there is great truth in this. When you think positively about something, things automatically energize themselves to make that happen. You know this fact in another form already probably – the Law of Attraction. Yes, this law can help you greatly in financially empowering yourself. Get acquainted with it today.

Conclusion

Financial empowerment is quite attainable, even if you have started with nothing. The fact is that most people don't think it can happen to them and hence they stay in the rut. One of the most important things to materialize the things mentioned in this eBook is that you have to have the faith in yourself. Believe that you can make the transition. Believe that you can take that leap.

The Family Budget Process

This brings us to the family budget process. We might ask questions like:

- How to set up a family budget?
- How should a family budget be used?

Insights around the tools and techniques of family budgeting could also be useful:

- Practical suggestions for setting up a budget?
- A step-by-step summary of a family budget process
- Hints, tips, tricks and tools for setting up a family budget

To get us started and in order to set up a monthly budget, follow these five easy steps:

Step one: find out your monthly take-home pay
Step two: find out what your expenses are
Step three: find out how much you spend on each expense
Step four: see if your monthly expenses match monthly take home pay
Step five: Balance your budget. This means in your family budget you need to ensure that you are spending matches take-home pay. It might indicate that you have to cut back on spending to balance.

It sounds too good to be true and too simplistic. However, in the end, that is all there is to this family budgeting process! Initially at least. Let us look at these steps one at a time.

Finding out your monthly take-home pay

Your income is your pay, after some money is deducted. Think taxes, insurance and Social Security. Answer the following questions:

What is your monthly take-home pay? Do other people share expenses in your home?

As mentioned before, total all of the households' monthly take home pay. This will include all sources of income for all contributing members of the household.

Finding out what your expenses are.

This brings up other pressing questions:

What are your monthly expenses? Where does the money in fact go every month?

Most people are surprised to learn that it may go for things that we do not need at all. Writing your expenditures down provides us with the unique opportunity to visualize and find out if any money goes for things that we do not need or want.

Here is a short list of expenses that many people have. Put a check mark next to ones you have, then write down any expenses you have, that are not on the list.

- Necessities like food.
- Clothes, laundry, dry-cleaning.
- Car and transportation expenses: gas, oil, parking, license, plates, car repair, train fare or bus fare.
- Rent, mortgage payments, heat, electricity, phone, water, property taxes, house repair, appliance and repair, furniture, small items for home, cleaning supplies on the yard care,
- Medical and dental expenses: doctor, dentist, drugs, hospital or clinic.
- Savings: short to medium term for something soon, a future purchase, emergencies, and investments.

- Installment payments: car, furniture, appliances, charge accounts, credit card accounts, and loans.
- Entertainment, movies, eating out, recreation, sports and equipment, club membership, newspaper, magazines, cable TV, records and tapes, DVDs videos and other multimedia, vacation, letters and postage.
- School bills, books, room and board at school, workshops, special training courses, lessons, music and more.
- Donations: church or synagogue, charitable giving, charities, other and gifts. Insurance: (if not deducted from your pay check): life, health, house, car and property.
- Taxes: (if not deducted from your pay check): Federal, state and local income, social security.

Which other ones could you list? Finding out how much you actually spend on each expense.

This is the hard part, where some thought and effort will have to go into the process to ensure the most accurate information is recorded. This will give a realistic and real-time estimate that is reliable and accurate.

In this section, you need to ask yourself how much each item on your list actually costs how much each item costs you a month.

The following estimates and guidelines could prove helpful to you as you set up your family budget:

- Monthly bills that stay the same – car and rental payments
- Monthly bills that change – utilities, phones and more. Find costs per month for say six months, add them up. Take this number you have calculated and divide it by six (the
- amount of months) to get your average cost. This is the number you will be using for your budgetary exercise.
- Bills that come every three or six months – the number for every month will be used in your budgetary process.
- Bills that come annually, meaning once a year – divide the amount by 12 months. The answer is your monthly budget number.
- Bills that come more than once a month – food, gas, lunch and family fun. This is a category to watch very closely, as it is a contributor to this "bottomless pit", we sometimes feel and see our cash disappear into.

- Unexpected expenditures or surprise bills – what you can afford to set aside as a buffer or emergency, contingency fund - (look at the last three years or so and see what kind of unexpected expenses you and your family faced). Use an estimate that makes sense to you and divide the annual number by twelve months to get your monthly number.
- Finding out if monthly expenses match monthly take-home pay.

Compare your total expenses with your take-home pay. A couple of results and scenarios could be staring you in the face:

Positive result: Income more than expense – you can either spend or save! Negative result: Expense more than income – spending more than you have, you might have to cut costs and try to save some money to cover the bases!

Whichever of these outcomes you are faced with, knowing is better than not knowing. For some this might bring little comfort and relief, but people in general, find this exercise useful to make an unknown more measurable. It makes us both accountable and wanting to act, faster and that sense of urgency and momentum is just what the family budget process needs!

Finding ways to balance your budget.
Earlier it was stated that a good budget would mean income would be equal to expenses. Having a small surplus is no guarantee by any means. You might need this to cover and unexpected rise in oil and gas prices or a larger grocery bill due to a party you are hosting at home. This almost brings the concept home of a sliding scale; flexibility and discretionary buffer categories in budgets to absorb this give-and-take roller coaster ride that is family budgeting.

The good news is whether you are in the red so to speak or just scraping by, managing to save nothing or maybe a little, or even a lot, this process will highlight areas where your attention is needed right away. It gives direction and purpose and assists families to formulate their spending plans, goals, re-visit their needs, dreams and goals.

Balancing the budget is no easy task. Here are a few steps that we can suggest to make your life a little easier:
- Find out how much you need to cut from your expenses.

- Decide you can make cuts in your expenses and be detailed.
- Re-balance your income and expenses after you've made these cuts.

A word to the wise: Do not make cuts in your budget that you cannot live with in real life. It is extremely important to remain realistic and keep your real-time expenses and living realities in the forefront of your mind when you make these decisions.

If you're getting out of a situation where you are in debt and short of cash, you have to try to curb spending any way you can. Cutting those expenses are crucial, not only because you are over budget. We mean that there might be other reasons, like adding a budget-line to your overall planning for your family vacation.

Realistically, we cannot add and address new needs and goals before we have fulfilled our duty and responsibilities. Cutting a little here and there will mostly do the trick – cancel that newspaper subscription for the papers that just land in the recycle box or garbage anyway. Do you need all the specialty channels and packages on your Cable TV options? Can you live with giving some up? There is always the specter of rising prices and interest rates, inflation and more to cope with as well, so building preparedness for that into your budget is also a priority. Whatever we can do to cut our costs and expenditure will benefit our pocketbooks and family budgets immensely!

Cutting back on things you need the least is a good starting point if you are at a total loss as to what and how to give something up, add a new line into your budget or plan for the future or inevitabilities. You are well on your way in the family budgeting process. You are doing it, every step of the way. Consolidate and re-visit your budget often – it is a dynamic process and "living" document or tools so to speak to help you keep your fingers on the pulse of your financial situation.

Another useful strategy is to set up a bill-paying plan and process that will protect your interest. When, how and how much you get paid will all influence your course of action. Creative and innovative allocation of your paycheck is the key. If you get paid once a month, the amounts in your budget will have to be paid monthly as is. If you get paid twice a month, divide each budget item by two. If paid bi-weekly (as is mostly the practice these days), still divide the monthly amount by two – it will not be the exact amount to plan for, but a rough and close estimate. In the end better than nothing!

If you are paid weekly, divide each budget item into 4. Cash flow management will form a big part of your fiscal strategy, once you have put your budget pen to paper and mapped out the needs and requirements. Utilize your cash, checking and savings account (if applicable) to pay for expenses. Do not pay your bills with your credit card! Keep track of all your discretionary spending. A financial diary for a week is always a good idea to scribble down in every time you withdraw money, pay for something or open your purse without thinking.

This will provide you with insights you did not have before on where the money actually goes. It will also carry within it, clues to adjust budget lines if actual cost is higher on certain items. Spending patterns and behaviors will emerge that might surprise or shock you!

Having some wriggle-room and discretionary spending is always motivation. The occasional treat and indulgence, special night out or other family activity is that more enjoyable, if you know you have worked hard to earn it and deserve a pat on the back for all your fiscal responsibility and discipline!

Always keep one eye on the future... budgets might need to change again and again for a variety of reasons. You can never feel you have "arrived" completely and that your budget

is set in stone. Family and life often throws us a curve ball or two, banks, service providers, government and fate sometimes

do too! Changing budgets should not be a source of frustration for you; it actually shows you that your family budgeting process is actually working. It is a real-time pulse and mechanism to capture these changes, which will leave you prepared and informed, ready to act and respond appropriately. This reason for change can come from different sources.

Here are some examples:

Change of income, goals, rising prices, goals reached, family growing, moving and or relocating to a new place, family getting smaller, new spending habits, change in lifestyle or unplanned expenses. If you can stick with it and see it through a family budget can help you meet your goals, get and stay out of debt, pay your bills on time, every time, keep track of your spending, cut costs and stretch your dollar to the max!

Now, use the following template to write out your family budget.

Monthly Income $_____
Expenses

_____	$_____
_____	$_____
_____	$_____
_____	$_____
_____	$_____
_____	$_____
_____	$_____
_____	$_____
_____	$_____
_____	$_____

Monthly Expenses Total $_____
Monthly   Income $_____   -
$_____Monthly Expenses
= $_____ Monthly Budget

I know that was a lot to digest, nevertheless it is very important for you family and your sanity. I wanted to be more entertaining in reading this chapter by the information is too valuable to your financial success to joke around.

If you don't do anything else, please fill out this monthly budget template. It will give you great insight on where you are financially. Take it a step further afterwards and work in expenses such as savings and investments. Good luck.

Starting Over Quotes

"With every rising of the sun
Think of your life as just begun."
-Ella Wheeler Wilcox

"Begin your life today, and again tomorrow."
- Jonathan Lockwood Huie

"So long as you have courage and a sense of humor, it is never too late to start life afresh."
- Freeman Dyson

"Re-examine all that you have been told...
dismiss that which insults your soul."
- Walt Whitman

"Stop holding on to the past.
Release your regrets about whatever you may have done or failed to do that turned out poorly.
Forgive others for whatever they may have done or failed to do that cause you harm.
Declare today to be a new beginning.
Let go of the past and move on with creating a joyful new future for yourself."
- Jonathan Lockwood Huie

"Though no one can go back and make a brand new start, anyone can start from now and make a brand new ending."

-Carl Bard

"You may have a fresh start any moment you choose, for this thing that we call 'failure' is not the falling down, but the stay down."

-Mary Pickford

"Never use your failure yesterday as an excuse for not trying again today. We may not be able to undo damages, but we can always make a new start."

-Unknown

"We cannot start over, but we can begin now, and make a new ending."

- Zig Ziglar

"It's never too late to be what you might have been."

-George Elliot

"You can't start the next chapter of your life if you keep re-reading the last one."

-Unknown

Positive Affirmations

Recite several of these every day to mentally stay strong and ready to take on what the world throws at you. Yes, I know at times it may feel silly or even weird. But if you commit to believing in you and working towards being life, these affirmations will make sense to you and you will happily commit to them.

- I am too big a gift too the world to waste my time on self-pity and sadness.
- I love and approve of myself.
- I take pleasure in my own solitude.
- I trust myself.
- I draw from my inner strength and light.
- I focus on breathing and grounding myself.
- My actions create constant prosperity.
- I am aligned with the energy of abundance.
- I am a unique child of this world.
- I accept responsibility if my anger for those who it has hurt.
- I forgive myself for all the mistakes I have made.
- I offer an apology to those affected by my anger.

- I let go of my anger so I can see clearly.
- I know my wisdom guides me to the right decision.
- I love my family even if they do not understand me completely.
- There is a good reason I was paired with this perfect family.
- I choose to see my family as a gift.
- I surround myself with people who treat me well.
- I never know what amazing incredible person I will meet next.
- Peaceful sleep awaits me in dreamland.
- I embrace the peace and quiet of the night.
- Today will be a gorgeous day to remember.
- I choose to fully participate in my day.
- I will let go of worries that drain my energy.
- I am in complete charge of planning for my future.
- I trust in my own ability to provide well for my family.
- I follow my dreams no matter what.
- I show compassion in helping my loved ones understand my dreams.
- I ask my loved ones to support my dreams.

- I accept everyone as they are and continue on with pursuing my dreams.
- All my problems have a solution.
- I attempt all – not some – possible ways to get unstuck.
- I seek a new way of thinking about this situation.
- I believe in my ability to unlock the way and set myself free.
- The answer is right before me, even if I am not seeing it yet.
- I compare myself only to my highest self.
- I am happy in my own skin and in my own circumstances.

Post Release Checklist

A list of things you need to obtain and secure prior to or immediately after your release.

Housing _____

Forwarding address _____

Email address _____

Contact phone number _____

Mentor or Counselor _____

Reliable transportation (Transit is good) _____

Church _____

Local Ex-Offender Advocacy Group _____

Locate a Library to use _____

Contact Supportive Friends_____

Contact Family Members _____

_____

_____

_____

_____

10 Helpful Resource Links

https://www.inmateaid.com

http://insidebooksproject.org/resource-guide/

http://www.helpforfelons.org

https://studentaid.ed.gov/sa/eligibility/criminal-convictions

http://www.legal-aid.org/en/home.aspx

http://georgiaopportunity.org

http://www.dca.state.ga.us/index.asp

http://pap.georgia.gov

http://www.georgiainnocenceproject.org

https://www.jobsforfelonshub.com

The Seven Essential Steps To A Successful Life

1. Your Vision

This is the most important step to being a more successful YOU. You can't proceed to the next step without clearly understand what it is that you want to accomplish. If you don't know what you want out of life, how can you attempt to better your life. Write down what you want out of life, going back to school, new career or retire early. Precisely write down the details of what you want and what it will take to achieve it.

2. Commitment

Commitment is more than just a word. Commitment is a decision and it requires action. Action that can't stop until the vision is a reality. Everyday you must do something that moves you closer to your vision.

3. Identify A Mentor

A mentor doesn't have to be someone famous or well known. The person you want to get advice from should be someone doing what is that you want to do or have accomplished what you want to accomplish. Your friends and family may love you but if they meet the qualification of a mentor like I just previously mentioned, don't take their advice.

4. Stay Positive
Whatever you are doing something important and positive, best believe negative people and negative energy will be attracted to you. Keep your mind and activities focused on positivity. Negative thoughts will slow your momentum towards your vision. Anytime you find yourself doubting your ability to make your vision a reality, think about how happy you will be and how wonderful your life will be, once your vision is achieved.

5. Enjoy Your Life
Through your process of turning your vision into a reality, take time to enjoy your life. Taking time to enjoy life will keep your life balanced while you go through the ups and downs of chasing your dreams.

6. Leave Your Comfort Zone
Step out of your comfort zone may sound like a cliché, but it is necessary. Your comfort zone is what you've been living in. You wouldn't have taken the time to list your vision or even be reading this book if you wanted to stay in your comfort zone. Like the saying goes, to get what

you've never had, you must do what you've never done.

7. Don't Be Afraid To Fail

We learn from failing. As babies, we would fall over and over again. However, we wouldn't have made it this far if as babies we didn't get back up, and eventually started walking. Each failure is an opportunity to learn, grow and make wiser choices.

The First 45 Days Journal

Keep a journal of your first 45 days of release. Jot down your plans for the day and then at the end of the day, document your process. Every day your efforts should lead you to the achieving the goals you will list below.

Top 3 Goals for the first 45 Days. You may have more than three goals but focus only on three. More than three goals will lead you in too many different directions. The first 45 days are very vital to your long time success. Take it serious and put in the work.

1. _____

2. _____

3. _____

Each day, read the previous day's entry to make sure you are on track with your goals. And yes, guys keep journals. Let's go.

Day 1

_____

_____

_____

_____

_____

_____

_____

_____

_____

_____

_____

_____

_____

_____

Day 2

_____

_____

_____

_____

_____

_____

_____

_____

_____

_____

_____

_____

Day 3

_____

_____

_____

_____

_____

_____

_____

_____

_____

_____

_____

_____

Day 4

Day 5

_____

_____

_____

_____

_____

_____

_____

_____

_____

_____

_____

_____

_____

_____

Day 6

Day 7

_____

_____

_____

_____

_____

_____

_____

_____

_____

_____

_____

_____

_____

Day 8

_____

_____

_____

_____

_____

_____

_____

_____

_____

_____

_____

_____

Day 9

_____

_____

_____

_____

_____

_____

_____

_____

_____

_____

_____

_____

Day 10

_____

_____

_____

_____

_____

_____

_____

_____

_____

_____

_____

_____

Day 11

_____

_____

_____

_____

_____

_____

_____

_____

_____

_____

_____

_____

_____

Day 12

_____

_____

_____

_____

_____

_____

_____

_____

_____

_____

_____

_____

Day 13

_____

_____

_____

_____

_____

_____

_____

_____

_____

_____

_____

_____

_____

_____

Day 14

_____

_____

_____

_____

_____

_____

_____

_____

_____

_____

_____

_____

Day 15

_____

_____

_____

_____

_____

_____

_____

_____

_____

_____

_____

_____

_____

Day 16

_____

_____

_____

_____

_____

_____

_____

_____

_____

_____

_____

_____

_____

Day 17

Day 18

Day 19

_____

_____

_____

_____

_____

_____

_____

_____

_____

_____

_____

_____

_____

Day 20

_____

_____

_____

_____

_____

_____

_____

_____

_____

_____

_____

_____

Day 21

_____

_____

_____

_____

_____

_____

_____

_____

_____

_____

_____

_____

Day 22

Day 23

_____

_____

_____

_____

_____

_____

_____

_____

_____

_____

_____

_____

_____

Day 24

_____

_____

_____

_____

_____

_____

_____

_____

_____

_____

_____

_____

Day 25

_____

_____

_____

_____

_____

_____

_____

_____

_____

_____

_____

_____

Day 26

Day 27

_____

_____

_____

_____

_____

_____

_____

_____

_____

_____

_____

_____

Day 28

_____

_____

_____

_____

_____

_____

_____

_____

_____

_____

_____

_____

_____

Day 29

_____

_____

_____

_____

_____

_____

_____

_____

_____

_____

_____

_____

Day 30

Day 31

_____

_____

_____

_____

_____

_____

_____

_____

_____

_____

_____

_____

_____

Day 32

Day 33

_____

_____

_____

_____

_____

_____

_____

_____

_____

_____

_____

_____

_____

Day 34

Day 35

Day 36

Day 37

_____

_____

_____

_____

_____

_____

_____

_____

_____

_____

_____

_____

_____

Day 38

Day 39

Day 40

_____

_____

_____

_____

_____

_____

_____

_____

_____

_____

_____

_____

_____

Day 41

_____

_____

_____

_____

_____

_____

_____

_____

_____

_____

_____

_____

_____

_____

Day 42

_____

_____

_____

_____

_____

_____

_____

_____

_____

_____

_____

_____

_____

Day 43

_____

_____

_____

_____

_____

_____

_____

_____

_____

_____

_____

_____

_____

_____

Day 44

Day 45

_____

_____

_____

_____

_____

_____

_____

_____

_____

_____

_____

_____

_____

The Author

After publishing his first book in 2013, Daddy Everyday: Rewriting the Black American Dad Story, Delonso Barnes entered the arena of public speaking and mentorship. Through his efforts, Barnes discovered that he has a passion for fatherhood— coming from the love and dedication he has for his own boys. The success of Daddy Everyday has inspired Barnes to form the non-profit organization Daddy Everyday Inc. Through this new entrepreneurial path; Barnes has fostered a fatherhood outreach program based in McDonough, Georgia. Daddy Everyday Inc. provides helpful advice for parents, empowering them with the necessary resources to help fathers to engage in family strengthening events & activities. Among Barnes' areas of focus include encouraging parents and students alike to support schools and educators— teaching fathers to become proactive in their children's education.

Contact Mr. Barnes at info@daddyeveryday.org

Bonus Improvement Tips

30-Day Challenge

The purpose of this 30-Day Challenge is to open your mind, heart and soul to the little changes you can do to make your overall life better. Each daily dare allows you to challenge yourself, escape your comfort zone, grow past your self-imposed limitations, and discover your skills and abilities. All challenges can help you grow as a parent or guardian. Now, I dare you to have the most fulfilling month of your life.

Day 1

Intro to what the 30 Day Dare is all about. MIRROR MIRROR. Look into a mirror, really look into a mirror. Try not to look at the fact you may need to shave or how one of your eyes is lower than the other. Tell yourself that you will be better, starting now. You can insert what you desire to be better at.

Day 2

Try something NEW, like a restaurant, radio station, or television show. The idea is to experience something you haven't. Initiate disruption in your comfort zone living. You can either try something new with your children or experience it by yourself.

Day 3

DAYDREAMING isn't just for kids; allow time to sit back and daydream, while thinking how you can make this a reality. After you finish daydreaming, take notes on things you can take action on now. Then take action.

Day 4

BE HEALTHY today. Only consume water and healthy foods for the day, you know what's good for you and what's not. Definitely include your family on this one and share the importance of it.

Day 5

Jot down the things you want, then ask yourself are you truly FOCUSED on getting these things. Let's say you want a new car or a new career. What steps are you taking to obtain these things?

Day 6

Create a PLAYLIST of your favorite songs that put you in a good mood, mix it up with different types of music. Play this playlist anytime you feel the need to energize yourself. Music is the answer.

Day 7

Everybody has a TALENT, whatever you are really good at. Demonstrate this talent the entire day to other people. You will enjoy the compliments. Sing, draw, or whatever; your kids will be inspired to discover and show their talents.

Day 8

UNPLUG today. No Facebook, no Twitter and no Internet Explorer. Spend the day reading a book, magazine, or just relax. No texts or calls either. This can be a weekend day or the whole weekend with the kids. Let them know there's life offline; you will see that as well.

Day 9

CALL someone you haven't talked to in a long time to reconnect or just to catch up. It seems simple, but think about all the times you meant to call someone. Today is the day. Heck, call a couple of people.

Day 10

RETURN TO INNOCENCE. Do things today that remind you of a time when life was simple. A time before growing up and things got complicated. Ride a bike, take a long walk in the park, play board games, or whatever reminds you of your earlier days.

Day 11

Get a good night SLEEP, your mind and body needs this, go to bed stress and worry free. This means 8 hours and going to bed with a clear mind. If you already get 8 hours, make sure to focus on going to bed without the negativity the world can sometimes hit you with.

Day 12

PLAN THE PERFECT WEEKEND, then figure out how you can make it happen, because it can with proper advance planning. Many of just fantasize about going on a dream vacation, not realizing it's possible with planning and budgeting.

Day 13

CHARITY. Do something as simple as donating your old clothes or food to a charity organization. You can even go as far as to get involved with an organization. This could be a valuable experience for your children to be a part of.

Day 14

SHARE a life experience with someone that can use it or just to people that may not know that about you. Talk to your kids about your life growing up. If you have a friend or co-worker going through one of life's tribulations, share with them how you got through it.

Day 15

Learn how to truly MEDIATE and practice it. Meditating will assist in getting you focused and finding happiness through inner peace.

Day 16

Take a look at your BODY IMAGE.
If you are not happy with it, do something about it. If you are happy with it, enjoy looking at yourself, and continue to maintain it.

Day 17

Step outside your COMFORT ZONE.
There are things you may want to do but they make you uncomfortable. Just do it. Think about going back to school, do some research or take a tour. Sing or perform poetry in front of an audience. Get comfortable getting out of your comfort zone.

Day 18

We all have a GUILTY PLEASURES; today enjoy it GUILT-FREE. Enjoy a cheesy sci-fi movie, have that double fudge chocolate chip cookie or jam to your favorite 80's music with the volume turned up. Whatever your guilty pleasure, enjoy it today.

Day 19

Are you where you want to be professionally? If not, then what's stopping you from your IDEAL PROFESSION? Once you answer that, determine if it is an excuse or a reason, there's a difference. Take a little time to do research and map out how you can make it a reality.

Day 20

Use your IMAGINATION. Think of creative ways to do things that you do everyday or get involved in something that allows you to explore your imagination. Consult with your kids on this one. Imagination is their specialty.

Day 21

SET DEADLINES, List whatever it is that you want to accomplish and add a completion by date next to each entry. Post it so you see it every day. It's time to get some things done.

Day 22

SAY I LOVE YOU, there are people in your life that you feel this way about but now you need to let them hear it.

Day 23

RESEARCH the things you want.
Whether it is returning to school, a change in your career, or learning how to be more productive, do the work to get a better understanding.

Day 24

ENCOURAGE others as well as yourself.
Being optimistic and spreading positive energy can be a powerful instrument in changing not only your life but the lives of others as well.

Day 25

List any BAD HABITS. This way you can admit the problem to yourself, which is the first step in fixing it. Take it to another level by writing what you are going to do to correct it next to each bad habit.

Day 26

JOIN A CLUB. Being around like-minded people is a great way to make new friends as well as to stay active. Go online and search organizations that have similar interests as you.

Day 27
CELEBRATE YOUR SUCCESS. You have made it this far in life so there are surely wins in your life worth recognizing. It's okay to pat yourself on the back sometimes.

Day 28
Take an intimate look into your finances, yes your MONEY. Create or revise your budget and determine what changes need to take place.

Day 29
Get ORGANIZED. There should be order in your life so you can be more productive and effective in what you do. Your car, your house, and pretty much everything in your life needs to be organized to create direction in your life.

Day 30
REVIEW your 30-Day Challenge Calendar and promise yourself to incorporate some of these challenges into your everyday life. Take a look at all the days that you had to write out a plan and review them.

Best of luck to you in your life's journey and visit DaddyEveryday.org for additional information on fatherhood. Also, remember that everyday is a chance at a Fresh Start.

Made in United States
Troutdale, OR
08/22/2023

12292089R00120